Shapes!

I See Circles

Elizabeth Lawrence

Cavendish Square

New York

Published in 2015 by Cavendish Square Publishing, LLC
243 5th Avenue, Suite 136, New York, NY 10016

Copyright © 2015 by Cavendish Square Publishing, LLC

First Edition

Library of Congress Cataloging-in-Publication Data

Lawrence, Elizabeth, 1988- author.
I see circles / Elizabeth Lawrence.
pages cm. — (Shapes!)
Includes index.
ISBN 978-1-50260-262-6 (hardcover) ISBN 978-1-50260-263-3 (paperback) ISBN 978-1-50260-266-4 (ebook)
1. Circle—Juvenile literature. 2. Shapes—Juvenile literature. 3. Geometry, Plane—Juvenile literature. I. Title.

QA484.L34 2015
516.15—dc23

2014024978

Editor: Kristen Susienka
Copy Editor: Cynthia Roby
Art Director: Jeffrey Talbot
Designer: Douglas Brooks
Senior Production Manager: Jennifer Ryder-Talbot
Production Editor: David McNamara
Photo Researcher: J8 Media

The photographs in this book are used by permission and through the courtesy of:
Cover photo by Influx Productions/Digital Vision/Getty Images; Sue Smith/Shutterstock.com, 5;
Africa Studio/Shutterstock.com, 7; Nacivet/Getty Images, 9; Tobik/Shutterstock.com, 11; NuntekulPhotography/Shutterstock.com, 13; John Giustina/Getty Images, 15;
Image Source/Getty Images, 17; SergiyN/iStock/Thinkstock, 19; Asier Romero/Shutterstock.com, 21.

Printed in the United States of America

Contents

Circles are all around us.

A **traffic light** has circles.

What colors are these circles?

5

You drink hot chocolate from a cup.

The top of the cup has a circle shape.

This circle is called a **rim**.

7

Sometimes people dig a hole to make a **well**.

The hole is shaped like a circle.

This well is deep and has water in it.

Do you like pizza?

This pizza is shaped like a circle.

How many circles are on top
of this pizza?

11

Circles are in your home and at your school.

Do you see a clock every day?

This clock is shaped like a circle.

13

Do you like to play games outdoors?

Some of your toys are shaped like circles.

A Frisbee is shaped like a circle.

Hockey is a game played on ice.

A hockey **puck** is shaped like a circle.

17

Our clothes have many shapes and **patterns**.

Polka dots are shaped like circles.

19

Circles are fun shapes!

See how many you can find around where you live.

New Words

patterns (PA-turns) Artistic forms, figures, or designs.

puck (PUCK) A rubber disk used to play hockey.

rim (RIM) The outer edge of something curved.

traffic light (TRA-fik LITE) A sign with red, yellow, and green lights that controls traffic.

well (WELL) A hole made in the earth to reach water, oil, or gas.

Index

23

About the Author

Elizabeth Lawrence lives in Albany, New York. She likes to write books, visit new places, and cook.

About

Bookworms help independent readers gain reading confidence through high-frequency words, simple sentences, and strong picture/text support. Each book explores a concept that helps children relate what they read to the world they live in.